Imperfect Posts

The Art and Psychology of Posting Like a Human

Rich Peterson

Generous Books

Contents

The Problem

You know the feeling.

You spend half an hour crafting a post. You rewrite the first line three times, trim the ending, add a photo, hit "publish"—and then wait.
A few likes trickle in. No comments. The post fades.
You think, *maybe I need to post more often or maybe I'm just not good at this.*

But deep down, you suspect something else:
It's not that your ideas aren't good.
It's that they don't feel *alive.*

You're not alone. Most people creating content today—freelancers, small businesses, even seasoned professionals—struggle with the same invisible barrier. Their words sound technically fine but emotionally flat. Their photos look polished but forgettable. Their videos explain everything yet connect with no one.

The problem isn't a lack of skill. It's the pursuit of perfection.

Why Perfection Fails

Perfection is seductive. It feels safe.
You polish, proof, edit, align, reframe; hoping to finally sound "professional."
But perfection also removes the very thing that makes people care: *texture.*

When every line sounds rehearsed and every image feels branded, the result is cold competence. People admire it, but they rarely respond to it.
Because the truth is: we don't interact with perfection. We interact with *personality.*

The Hidden Truth About Social Media

You've been told engagement depends on trends, timing or algorithms.
But long before there were algorithms, there was psychology.

Every "like," "comment," and "share" is still driven by the same human impulses that existed around campfires and coffee tables:

- Reciprocity — "You gave me something; I want to give back."
- Identity — "This reflects who I am."
- Emotion — "This made me feel something real."
- Curiosity — "I need to see how this ends."

The problem isn't that social media changed people. It's that it made people forget how people work.

What This Book Is About

Imperfect Posts is a book about returning to that human core. It's about how to write, speak and show up online in a way that sounds *alive* again, without resorting to clickbait, trends or robotic polish.

You'll learn:

- Why imperfection builds trust faster than precision.
- How to make your posts emotionally textured—varied, real and resonant.
- How to use psychology, not formulas, to create natural interaction.
- And how to experiment fearlessly, even when you're not sure what will work.

This isn't a book about performing better.
It's a book about **connecting deeper.**

Who This Book Is For

This book is for freelancers, small business owners and creators who want to post online but feel uneasy doing it.
For people who love their work but hate how "content creation" has made it feel mechanical.
For anyone who's ever said:

> "I want to post but I don't want to sound fake."

If you've ever worried you're "too normal," "too boring" or "too human" for social media—this book is your permission slip.

What You'll Take Away

By the end of this book, you'll have:

- A deep understanding of the *psychology of genuine engagement.*
- A toolkit for crafting text, visuals and stories that resonate naturally.
- A mindset shift from *perfection and performance* to *connection and experimentation.*

You'll stop chasing content that "works" and start creating posts that **feel alive;** because they reflect the real, imperfect person behind them.

How to Use This Book

Each chapter builds from insight → skill → application.

- The early sections explain why perfection fails and what drives human interaction.
- The middle chapters show how to write, design and tell stories that feel genuine.
- The final chapters help you build consistency, confidence and creative rhythm—without losing your voice.

You can read it straight through or dip into specific chapters when you feel stuck.
Every section stands on its own, but together, they form a human approach to creating content that connects.

The Reader's Contract

If you read with curiosity and apply what you learn, this book will change the way you post.
You'll:

- Understand why people truly interact with content.
- Develop your own texture and tone.
- Learn to experiment safely and confidently.
- And most importantly, you'll rediscover the *joy* of creating.

I can't promise virality.
But I can promise that by the end, you'll post in a way that feels like **you**—and that's the most magnetic strategy there is.

Chapter 1: The Silence Between Posts

Why the Room Feels Empty

You post something you care about.
You've thought about it, edited it, rewritten the first line three times. It sounds good. It even looks good. You press "publish" — and then nothing.
A few likes, maybe a kind comment from a friend. Then silence.

That silence hurts in a way that's hard to explain.
It feels personal, even when you know it's not. You tell yourself, *"It's just the algorithm,"* but deep down, you wonder if maybe it's you — your tone, your words, your ideas.

You're not imagining it. Something *is* missing.
It's not your effort. It's your energy.
What your post lacks isn't correctness, it's connection.

The Hidden Emotion Behind Engagement

Every interaction — a like, a comment, a save — is a small emotional decision. People don't engage with logic. They engage when something stirs a feeling: recognition, empathy, curiosity, gratitude, surprise.

That means every piece of content has a hidden layer underneath the words or images — a pulse of *emotional intention.*

When you post just to inform, you're sending information.
When you post to connect, you're extending emotion.

That difference sounds subtle, but it's everything.
The first approach is a transaction: *"Here's knowledge."*
The second is a conversation: *"Here's how this felt."*

Why "Perfect" Feels Distant

You've probably been told that quality matters. That you should post polished, professional content. But in most cases, polish is where personality goes to die.

Perfection hides your humanness.
When every sentence sounds measured, the reader senses restraint, not sincerity.
When your image looks flawless, it says *"crafted,"* not *"lived."*

The human mind detects this instantly, we're wired to notice dissonance. We can feel when something looks right but doesn't *feel* real.
That's why people scroll past "perfect" content but pause on the imperfect. The imperfect feels safe. It feels like *us.*

The Unspoken Barrier

The silence between your posts isn't disinterest, it's disconnection.
People scroll past because they don't sense you.

The instinct to over-perfect comes from protection. You polish because you care. You edit because you respect your reader. You refine because you don't want to waste attention.
But the irony is: the more you perfect your message, the more you remove yourself from it.

Polish creates distance.
And distance kills empathy.
Empathy is what compels response.

The Moment Before Someone Interacts

Here's what happens in the instant before someone decides to engage with your content:

1. **Recognition:** "This feels like me."

2. **Emotion:** "This makes me feel something."

3. **Permission:** "It's safe to react."

No one interacts because they "should."
They interact because something inside them stirs, and that spark of emotion feels personal.

You don't need to create viral content.
You need to create *moments of recognition.*

The First Small Shift

Try this the next time you write a post:
Before you edit, pause and ask,

"Does this sound like a person or a presentation?"

If it sounds like something you'd say out loud, you're close.
If it sounds like something you'd *read at a meeting*, you've gone too far.

Most people think improvement comes from removing mistakes.
In truth, it comes from restoring emotion.
That's the first step toward posts that feel alive.

Key Takeaways

- Silence online doesn't mean people don't care — it means they don't *feel* yet.
- Perfection hides personality; imperfection creates trust.
- Emotion, not information, drives engagement.
- You don't need to post "better" — you need to post more *humanly.*

Reflection Prompt

Think of the last post you wrote that mattered to you.
If you stripped out every "should," every polish, every performance — what would it sound like?
That's where your real voice is hiding.

Next Chapter: "The Hidden Cost of Polished" — where we explore the psychology behind why too much perfection repels attention and how small imperfections actually *increase* credibility and emotional warmth.

Chapter 2: The Hidden Cost of Polished

Why "Professional" Isn't Always Persuasive

At some point, most of us were told that if we want to be taken seriously, we need to look professional.
Use clean visuals. Tight copy. Flawless grammar.
And for a while, that worked.

But something changed.

In a world where everyone learned the same rules, how to crop an image, use a template or follow a tone guide, everything started to look and sound the same.
Polish became the new beige.
And beige doesn't make people feel anything.

When everything looks "right," it all starts to feel *wrongly familiar.*
It feels mass-produced, even when it isn't.

The Psychology of Over-Polish

Humans are hardwired to seek warmth and authenticity. We connect with signs of humanness; imperfections that signal honesty, emotion and presence.

When a post feels too perfect, our subconscious brain interprets it as *calculated.*
It triggers scepticism instead of trust.
We don't mean to, it's an automatic defence.

Behavioural researchers call this **the effort-accuracy tradeoff**: when something feels over-engineered, the mind assumes the intent is persuasion, not communication.
It's a built-in suspicion filter, protection against being sold to.

And that's the hidden cost of polish:
It makes people admire you, not relate to you.

The Cognitive Friction That Creates Trust

There's a concept in psychology called **cognitive fluency**; how easily information is processed by the brain. Generally, the easier something is to understand, the more we trust it. But here's the twist: if something is *too easy,* too clean, too smooth, too symmetrical, it feels artificial.

Small imperfections create **cognitive friction**: a subtle bump in our processing that tells our brain,

> "This is real. This was made by a person."

That's why we're drawn to handwritten notes, voice cracks, imperfect lighting or small hesitations in speech.
They're not mistakes — they're signals of sincerity.

In content, those same micro-imperfections, the conversational "ums," the slightly uneven photo, the imperfect sentence rhythm, act as proof of life.

The Handmade Effect

Think about the difference between a factory-made mug and one made by a potter.
The first is flawless; smooth, symmetrical, functional.
The second might wobble slightly, with fingerprints pressed into the glaze.
Most people instinctively choose the handmade mug, even if both hold coffee equally well.

That's called the **handmade effect** — when evidence of human effort increases emotional value.
We don't just buy the mug.
We buy the story, the touch, the imperfection that makes it unique.

Posts work the same way. When people can sense your hand in the work — your rhythm, your quirks, your uneven brilliance — they feel safe enough to engage.
They stop scrolling not because it's perfect, but because it's *personal.*

Why "Good Enough" Often Works Better

Perfection is costly, not just in time, but in energy.
Every hour spent polishing one piece is an hour *not spent sharing another story.*

Good content creators iterate. Great ones connect.
The difference? They're willing to post before it's flawless.

The creators you admire most aren't perfect; they're prolific. Their rhythm builds trust more than their precision ever could. Their imperfection signals motion, and motion feels alive.

Try This: The 80% Rule

Before posting, ask yourself:

> "If this post were 80% ready — but felt 100% honest — would I still share it?"

If the answer is yes, you're ready.
The remaining 20% of polish won't make it more engaging, it'll just make it safer.
And safety is invisible online.

Your audience isn't looking for a final draft; they're looking for a *fellow traveller.*

Key Takeaways

- Polish creates admiration, but imperfection creates trust.
- The human brain connects faster to warmth than to precision.
- Small imperfections act as "proof of life" — evidence of emotion and honesty.

- The goal isn't to look perfect; it's to feel *present.*
- Post at 80% finished if it's 100% real.

Reflection Prompt

Think of a time you connected deeply with someone else's post or story.
Was it perfect? Or was it honest, maybe even a little messy?
Now ask: how can you bring that same humanity into your next piece of content?

Next Chapter: "The Algorithm Is Human Nature" — where we explore why human psychology, not technology, has always driven engagement — and how to design content around timeless social instincts.

Chapter 3: The Algorithm Is Human Nature

The Myth of the Machine

Every time a post underperforms, someone blames "the algorithm."
It's an easy villain — invisible, changing and seemingly unfair.

But here's the uncomfortable truth: algorithms don't create behaviour; they **mirror it.**
Every change, every tweak, every trend that rises or fades — it all reflects what people already do, want and feel.

When someone scrolls, pauses, likes or comments, that data becomes the algorithm's new rule.
In other words: it isn't leading us, it's following us.

So when we say *"the algorithm didn't show my post,"* what we're really saying is:

> "The emotion in my post didn't spread."

That's not a system problem.
That's a human one.

The Real Engine of Engagement

Behind every like, share or comment lies a tiny emotional spark — a moment of human connection translated into digital motion.

Psychologists call these **micro-reciprocities**:
the small emotional exchanges that happen when we feel seen, informed or inspired.

These are the ancient engines of attention; the same ones that powered storytelling, gossip and word-of-mouth long before the internet existed.

They're built on four timeless instincts:

1. **Reciprocity** – When we receive, we want to give back.
   → "You gave me something of value. I'll engage to return the favor."

2. **Curiosity** – When something teases the unknown, we can't look away.
   → "What happens next?"

3. **Identity** – When content reinforces who we are (or who we want to be), we interact.
   → "This feels like me."

4. **Emotion** – When something makes us *feel*, we signal that feeling through interaction.
   → "I have to respond to this."

Every algorithm ever designed amplifies these same principles because these are what people amplify.

Why Technology Keeps Repeating Human Behaviour

Trends come and go, but if you look closely, they all follow the same human loop:

1. **Discovery:** Something new sparks curiosity.
2. **Connection:** Early adopters bond over shared enthusiasm.
3. **Performance:** People copy what works, polish it and repeat it.
4. **Decay:** The repetition kills curiosity, and the crowd moves on.

We call it "content fatigue." But really, it's **emotional adaptation.**
When a stimulus stops surprising us, it stops rewarding us.

So, no matter how the platforms change, the laws of engagement stay constant:

- Surprise me.
- Make me feel something.
- Let me belong.

Designing for People, Not Platforms

Once you stop fighting the algorithm, you can design *for humans instead of systems.*

That means asking:

- What emotion do I want someone to feel here?
- What tiny gift am I giving them — insight, humour, validation, beauty?
- How can I make this feel alive, not automated?

If you answer those, the metrics take care of themselves.
Because the best "algorithm strategy" is empathy.

The Predictable Nature of Surprise

Ironically, the only thing that consistently wins online is *genuine surprise.*
We're wired for novelty. When something feels slightly new, unexpected or emotionally unpredictable, our attention wakes up.

That's why imperfect posts — the unpolished ones, the spontaneous ones — travel further.
They contain **emotional entropy;** the small uncertainty that makes people pay attention.
It's not chaos. It's human reality.

And every algorithm, no matter how advanced, is always looking for the same signal:

> "Did people care enough to react?"

If they did, the algorithm spreads it, because people already have.

You Don't Need to Be Strategic, You Need to Be Human

Every content strategy eventually becomes obsolete.
But empathy, generosity, curiosity and emotional truth?
They don't expire.

Algorithms will evolve for decades, but they'll always be trained on human data — which means they'll always chase what we chase: emotion, meaning and belonging.

So, the only sustainable strategy is this:

> Post things that move *you* first.
> If it moves you, it will move someone else.

The systems might change.
Human nature won't.

Key Takeaways

- Algorithms don't decide what people like — they *learn* it from people.
- Engagement runs on timeless human instincts: reciprocity, curiosity, identity and emotion.
- If your content sparks emotion or recognition, algorithms will amplify it naturally.
- Stop optimising for systems; design for psychology.

- Imperfection triggers attention because it feels real — not rehearsed.

Reflection Prompt

Think of a post that unexpectedly performed well — maybe something you made casually or imperfectly. Ask yourself:
Which of the four instincts did it trigger?
Now, instead of copying the format, recreate the *feeling.*

Next Chapter: "How Attention Actually Works" — where we break down the micro-moments of focus and feeling that turn a simple scroll into genuine engagement and how to design content that earns—not demands—attention.

Chapter 4: How Attention Actually Works

The Split Second That Decides Everything

When someone scrolls past your post, it's easy to assume they didn't care.
But the truth is more precise — they didn't *feel* fast enough.

Every moment online is a competition for mental energy.
In the first fraction of a second, the brain performs a rapid, unconscious check:

> "Is this relevant to me?"
> "Does it feel safe or interesting?"
> "Should I give it more energy?"

These questions happen below awareness.
By the time someone "decides" to engage, their body already has.

Attention, then, isn't a button we press — it's a reflex we earn.
And the reflex responds not to cleverness, but to *emotional clarity.*

The Attention Ladder

Imagine attention as a small ladder your reader climbs one rung at a time:

1. **Notice:** "Something here caught my eye."
2. **Pause:** "I think this might matter."
3. **Feel:** "This resonates with me."
4. **Decide:** "I'll give it my time."
5. **Act:** "I'll comment, share or remember this."

Most content never gets people past the first rung — they notice, then keep scrolling.
The best content carries them all the way up.
And the key to that climb isn't novelty, it's *neural efficiency.*

When content feels emotionally or visually *familiar enough* to process easily, yet *different enough* to spark curiosity, it keeps people climbing.

That delicate balance, between recognition and surprise, is the heart of attention.

What the Brain Really Wants

Neuroscientists describe attention as an economy of prediction. The brain saves energy by focusing on things that either:

- **Confirm what it values** (identity, belonging, shared truth) or

- **Violate what it expects** (curiosity, humour, surprise).

That means attention isn't random. It's deeply personal.
Every like or comment says, in essence,

> "This content fits my story — or disrupts it in an interesting way."

Your job as a creator isn't to shout louder.
It's to whisper something that feels unmistakably human — something that makes a reader's mind lean closer.

The Feeling of Relevance

Relevance isn't just topical; it's emotional.
A photo of a coffee cup can be deeply relevant if it carries a relatable moment: exhaustion, comfort, reflection.

To design for attention, ask:

> "What emotional state does this post live in?"

Joy, frustration, gratitude, nostalgia; these are the currencies of relevance.
The brain doesn't sort posts by format; it sorts them by *feeling.*

A human scrolls not to consume, but to connect.

How to Make People Pause

You can't force someone to stop scrolling, but you can make them curious enough to want to.
Try this sequence when shaping your content:

1. **Start with empathy.** Open with something *known* — a shared truth or moment.

2. **Add curiosity.** Introduce a small twist or emotional tension.

3. **Deliver humanity.** End with vulnerability, insight or a touch of warmth.

This creates a natural arc: recognition → tension → emotion → resolution.
It's how stories work, how attention flows and how humans decide to care.

The Problem with Demanding Attention

Many creators try to force attention: louder headlines, bolder claims, higher frequency.
It works briefly, and then burns out.
Forced attention drains trust because it trades sincerity for spectacle.

Earned attention, by contrast, builds trust because it feels respectful.
It says, *"I see you, and I made this for you."*
That's the kind of attention people return to.

Practical Cue: The 3-Second Test

Before you post, look at your draft and ask:

> "If someone saw this for three seconds, would they *feel* something — or just *see* something?"

If it's the latter, dig deeper.
Add one moment of truth: a phrase, a detail or a shift in tone that humanises it.
Even a single sentence of vulnerability changes everything.

Key Takeaways

- Attention is an emotional reflex, not a rational decision.
- The brain focuses on what feels both familiar and fresh.
- Relevance is emotional before it's topical.
- Earned attention feels like empathy; forced attention feels like noise.
- The simplest test: Does this post make someone *feel* something within three seconds?

Reflection Prompt

Think of the last time you stopped scrolling.
What was the exact moment that made you pause?

Write down the emotion it stirred — that emotion is your next creative starting point.

Next Chapter: "Goodwill — The Hidden Currency of Engagement" — where we explore why the instinct to give freely (through value, warmth or vulnerability) is the most powerful way to earn sustainable interaction.

Chapter 5: Goodwill — The Hidden Currency of Engagement

The Invisible Exchange

Every time someone interacts with your content — liking, commenting, saving or sharing — they're not just reacting. They're reciprocating.

They're saying,

> "You gave me something that made me feel something."

In that moment, something invisible changes hands: **goodwill.**

Goodwill is the emotional credit that builds when you consistently offer genuine value; a thought that helps, a story that comforts, a truth that resonates.
It's not transactional. It's relational.
And over time, it becomes the most powerful driver of engagement you have.

The Psychology of Giving First

In behavioural psychology, the **norm of reciprocity** is one of the most universal social rules. When someone gives to us — a gift, a favour, an idea, even attention — we feel a quiet urge to give something back.

It's not obligation; it's balance.

That's why generosity, in any form, feels magnetic online. When your post gives — a moment of recognition, a piece of insight, a spark of humour — readers instinctively want to repay it: with a comment, a share, a memory.

It's also why self-promotional content fails. When every post asks without offering, it breaks the emotional symmetry. It makes people feel used instead of seen.

The most engaged creators aren't shouting louder. They're giving better.

What "Value" Really Means

Most people hear "give value" and think "teach something." But value isn't just information, it's an *emotionally useful experience.*

Here are five forms of value that build goodwill:

1. **Clarity** – Simplifying something confusing.
2. **Comfort** – Helping people feel less alone in what they're feeling.

3. **Curiosity** – Offering a fresh angle or question that wakes people up.

4. **Challenge** – Gently disrupting a comfortable assumption.

5. **Cheer** – Adding levity or hope in a noisy, serious world.

Each form gives your audience a small win, and that win becomes trust.

The Emotional Bank Account

Think of your relationship with your audience as an emotional bank.
Every generous post deposits goodwill. Every self-serving one withdraws it.
The goal isn't to avoid withdrawals — it's to maintain a healthy balance.

When goodwill is high:

- People forgive small mistakes.
- They engage even when your topic shifts.
- They assume good intent.

When goodwill is low:

- Every post feels like a pitch.
- Engagement drops even when quality rises.
- People scroll past because they've stopped expecting

sincerity.

The solution isn't more polish, it's more generosity.

How to Design for Goodwill

1. **Ask: "What's the gift here?"**
   Before posting, identify one small thing the reader gains — insight, emotion, clarity, comfort.

2. **Remove hidden asks.**
   If your post says "click," "buy," "follow," or "share" more than once, it's asking too much.

3. **Let vulnerability lead.**
   Honesty is generosity. When you share your learning moments, readers get to see themselves in your story.

4. **Be emotionally specific.**
   Vague positivity ("Be kind!") fades fast. Specific emotions ("Yesterday I nearly gave up, but this helped.") create memory.

5. **Show warmth without performance.**
   Genuine care shows in rhythm, not emojis.

The Reciprocity Loop

Goodwill creates a loop — a virtuous cycle of giving and receiving.

1. You share something real.

2. Someone resonates and responds.

3. That response affirms you, inspiring another post.

4. The cycle repeats — now with trust at the centre.

That's how communities form organically. Not through automation, but through mutual emotional generosity.

Goodwill compounds. Every post builds a little more of it — and every act of generosity makes the next one easier.

Why This Is the Only Sustainable Strategy

You can outsmart an algorithm once. You can't outsmart human emotion.
Tactics fade; goodwill endures.

When you post from goodwill — when your motivation is to help, not perform — people can *feel it.*
That feeling is contagious. It travels through shares, comments and quiet appreciation you'll never even see.

The truth is, your most loyal audience isn't built in public. It's built in private — in the silent thank-yous people feel when your post made their day slightly better.

Key Takeaways

- Goodwill is emotional credit — earned through consistent generosity.

- Reciprocity drives engagement more reliably than any algorithm.

- Value isn't information — it's emotional usefulness.

- Vulnerability and warmth are the strongest deposits you can make.
- When you give first, connection becomes effortless.

Reflection Prompt

Think of a post that gave you something intangible — a laugh, an idea, a sigh of relief.
What made it feel like a gift rather than a demand?
Now, look at your drafts.
Where could you add that same sense of giving?

Next Chapter: "The Power of Emotional Texture" — where we explore how tone, pacing and emotional variety make content feel alive and how to build rhythm that keeps people coming back.

Chapter 6: The Power of Emotional Texture

Why Flat Posts Fall Flat

Sometimes a post is perfect on paper.
It's clear, polished, useful — yet something about it feels... empty.

Readers understand it, but they don't *feel* it.
It's like music played at a perfect tempo but without dynamics — technically flawless, emotionally monotone.

That's because emotion isn't just *what* you say. It's *how* it feels in rhythm, tone and contrast.

The difference between a post that sounds professional and one that sounds *alive* comes down to one thing: **texture.**

What "Texture" Actually Means

Texture is the variety and rhythm of emotion in your content — the push and pull between intensity and calm, sincerity and wit, story and statement.

It's what gives a reader's brain tiny spikes of contrast, which the mind translates as *interest.*

Just as a piece of music alternates between loud and soft or a conversation flows between serious and light, textured content keeps people engaged because it mirrors the *way real humans express themselves.*

Without texture, your content becomes emotionally flat.
With texture, it feels *alive, unpredictable and true.*

The Psychology of Contrast

The human brain is wired to notice change.
In neuroscience, this is called **novelty detection** — a built-in alert system that wakes up when something shifts in tone or pattern.

When your writing moves between emotions — from humour to honesty, simplicity to depth — you're giving the reader's brain a natural rhythm to follow.
It feels organic because it mirrors how emotion moves in real life.

Perfectly consistent tone signals control.
Varied tone signals humanity.

And humans trust humanity.

Why Smooth Feels Forgettable

Most creators remove texture by accident.
They smooth out their sentences to sound "professional."
They flatten humour to avoid risk.
They trim emotions to sound polished.

But that's like sanding every surface in a home until it loses warmth.

A little unevenness — a sharp phrase, a soft pause, an unexpected confession — is what makes content memorable.

Smooth posts make sense.
Textured posts make *impact.*

The Texture Spectrum

Here's how to think about emotional texture in your own content.
Across your posts, vary the mix of these emotional tones:

Tone Type	Emotion Evoked	Example Use
Raw	Vulnerability, trust	"I nearly gave up this week..."
Reflective	Connection, meaning	"Here's what that moment taught me."
Playful	Warmth, approachability	"Let's admit it, we've all done this."
Practical	Clarity, action	"Here's the simple way I fixed it."
Provocative	Curiosity, disruption	"What if we've been doing this wrong?"

The goal isn't to use every tone in one post.
It's to let your content body of work have **range** — like a well-balanced conversation across time.

Microtexture: Inside a Single Post

Even within a single piece, you can use texture to shape emotion:

- **Rhythm:** Mix short and long sentences.
- **Spacing:** Use line breaks to add breath.

- **Pacing:** Alternate between detail and simplicity.
- **Tone:** Pair honesty with levity.

Texture isn't noise, it's musicality.
It's how the emotional *melody* of your post unfolds.

How Texture Builds Connection

When people say a creator "feels real," they're usually responding to texture.
It's not that the creator is more authentic; it's that their work *feels lived in.*

A textured voice communicates more than ideas — it communicates *emotion in motion.*
That motion is what keeps readers close.

Flat content ends conversations.
Textured content starts them.

Practical Cue: The Contrast Check

Before publishing, ask:

> "Where does this post change emotional temperature?"

If it doesn't shift tone even once — from light to serious or from teaching to feeling — it might be too even.
Add one turn of contrast: a human aside, a moment of laughter or a line of silence.

Your reader's attention will follow wherever your emotion leads.

Key Takeaways

- Texture is emotional contrast — the rhythm of light and shadow in your tone.
- The brain notices change more than perfection.
- Consistent tone feels safe but sterile; varied tone feels human and alive.
- Use rhythm, pacing and emotional shifts to keep readers engaged.
- A post without texture reads like a manual. A post with texture feels like a memory.

Reflection Prompt

Think of one creator whose content you *feel* more than you just understand.
What do they do that adds texture — tone shifts, rhythm, vulnerability, humour?
How can you borrow that technique in your next post while staying true to your own voice?

Next Chapter: "Writing That Sounds Like a Person" — where we turn texture into craft by exploring how to write conversationally, intuitively and with emotional rhythm — the foundation of human-sounding content.

Chapter 7: Writing That Sounds Like a Person

The Irony of Writing Online

Most people sound more human in a 10-second voice note than in a 200-word post.
In person, they're animated, funny, messy; full of pauses and half-sentences that somehow make perfect sense.
Then they sit down to write and transform it into a corporate press release.

It's not their fault.
We were trained to write to impress, not to connect.
But connection is the new professionalism.
And sounding human is the new credibility.

Why "Good Writing" Often Sounds Wrong

You've probably internalised a few myths about writing:

- Good writing is grammatically perfect.
- Every sentence must sound polished.
- Emotion makes you look unprofessional.

Those rules work for essays, but not for conversations.
And posting online is a conversation.

Human attention isn't drawn to correctness, it's drawn to *recognition.*
We engage when something sounds like a person, not a persona.

So your job isn't to write better.
It's to write closer to how you *think* and *feel.*

The Psychology of Voice

Language is emotional code.
When you read someone's words, your brain automatically recreates their tone, pace and facial expression.
This is called **subvocalization** — we "hear" the writer's voice in our head.

That's why robotic phrasing breaks connection: it gives the brain nothing human to simulate.
Conversational writing, by contrast, activates empathy.
It feels like dialogue — even though you're the only one speaking.

If your words sound like they came from a person your reader would actually enjoy having coffee with, you're doing it right.

How to Sound Like Yourself (Again)

1. **Write the way you'd say it.**
   Record yourself explaining your idea to a friend. Transcribe it. Edit lightly for clarity, not polish.

2. **Use "you" and "I."**
   Posts without pronouns sound like lectures. Posts with

pronouns sound like relationships.

3. **Skip the filler.**
   Phrases like "In today's fast-paced world" or "I wanted to take a moment to share" create distance. Start where it feels real.

4. **Read it out loud.**
   If it sounds stiff when spoken, it will read stiff. Your ear catches what your eyes ignore.

5. **Don't remove all quirks.**
   A few incomplete sentences. A stray "honestly." A shift in rhythm. These are signs of life. Keep them.

Conversational Rhythm

People don't talk in long, even sentences.
We start, stop, emphasise, trail off, double back.
That natural rhythm is what makes voice *feel alive.*

You can mimic that in writing by varying:

- **Sentence length:** Short sentences create urgency. Long ones create flow. Mix both.
- **Punctuation:** Use dashes and ellipses sparingly — they simulate breath and thought.
- **Line breaks:** Each break adds a micro-pause, helping readers *feel* the cadence of speech.

Rhythm is how you make a reader *hear* you.

The Tone Triangle

Think of every post as a small triangle balancing three tones:

Tone	Purpose	Example
Warm	Builds connection and trust.	"You've probably felt this too."
Clear	Builds credibility.	"Here's what actually works."
Real	Builds emotional intimacy.	"Yesterday, I nearly quit."

Too much warmth feels soft.
Too much clarity feels cold.
Too much "real" feels heavy.
Blend the three? Your reader feels safe, informed and understood.

Human Error as Style

A small typo. An unplanned repetition. A slightly odd phrase. These don't ruin posts, they remind people a person wrote them.

Perfection signals automation.
Human error signals honesty.

The trick is to stay on the line between casual and careless.
If your tone feels intentional, even a broken sentence feels artistic.

Practical Cue: The Mirror Test

After writing your post, ask:

> "If I said this out loud to someone I respect, would it sound natural?"

If not, strip away the polish until it does.
That's your real voice.

Key Takeaways

- The most engaging writing sounds spoken, not scripted.
- Readers hear your tone subconsciously — make it sound alive.
- Quirks, rhythm and warmth create trust faster than grammar.
- Mix warmth, clarity and realism for emotional balance.
- Imperfection isn't unprofessional; it's relatable.

Reflection Prompt

Open your last post.
Now read it aloud as if you were telling it to someone you like and trust.
Where does it feel too stiff or distant?
That's where your next edit begins.

Next Chapter: "Visuals That Feel Real" — where we explore how authenticity in imagery and design works the same way: people don't trust what looks perfect; they trust what feels *lived in.*

Chapter 8: Visuals That Feel Real

The Problem With Pretty

You've seen them: the glossy flat-lay photos, perfect lighting, perfectly balanced colour palette, the "on-brand" look.
They're nice.
They're also forgettable.

The human brain isn't wired to bond with "nice." It bonds with *real.*

In a feed full of perfection, authenticity looks like rebellion.
A slightly blurry photo. A raw sketch. A behind-the-scenes moment.
These are what people stop for, because they hint at truth.

Polish creates admiration.
Imperfection creates connection.

The Psychology of Visual Honesty

People subconsciously read visuals the same way they read faces. We're constantly scanning for **emotion and intent** — looking for signals of trust, warmth and relatability.

When something feels overly edited, our brain registers it as **managed emotion**, the visual version of a script.
But when we see a slightly crooked photo, natural light, a real environment, our brain recognises *life.*
It says,

"Someone was there."

That's the moment connection happens.
You've replaced design with *presence.*

The Handmade Effect (Again)

In Chapter 2, we talked about the handmade effect, the idea that people value human traces.
It applies doubly to visuals.

Psychologists studying aesthetic preference have found that **imperfections in craft** — brushstrokes, pencil marks, irregular edges — trigger empathy and curiosity. They remind us that *a person* made this.

The same holds true digitally.
Your hand in the frame. Your messy desk. Your sketchy whiteboard.
These aren't distractions. They're emotional bridges.

They whisper: *This is real life, not a brand campaign.*

The Hidden Power of Framing

Composition is emotional language.
Every decision — where you place yourself, how much space you leave, what you crop — tells the viewer how to feel.

- **Tight framing** (close-up) says: *I want you to feel what I feel.*
- **Wide framing** says: *I want you to see what I see.*
- **Unbalanced framing** says: *This is happening in real time.*

Perfect symmetry feels designed.
Asymmetry feels lived.

Try thinking less like a designer and more like a documentarian: your goal isn't to *present*, it's to *witness.*

Colour, Light and Emotion

Visuals carry emotional temperature.
Warm light feels intimate. Cool tones feel distant.
High contrast feels dramatic. Low contrast feels calm.

The key is to let your visuals match the **emotional truth** of your post.

If your story is personal, keep the tone soft and natural.
If it's bold or challenging, use sharper lines and higher contrast.
The goal isn't aesthetic perfection; it's emotional coherence.

When your visuals and emotions align, people don't just see your post — they *feel* it.

The Trap of Consistency

Brands are told to maintain visual consistency — the same colours, fonts, styles.
Consistency builds recognition, yes — but sameness breeds indifference.

Humans crave **recognisable variety** — enough familiarity to feel safe, enough change to stay interested.

Let your visuals evolve like seasons: connected by tone, not template.
That's what real life looks like.

Practical Cue: The "Human in the Frame" Rule

Before you post an image, ask:

> "Can a human trace be felt here?"

It doesn't always mean showing your face.
It could be a hand, a handwritten note, a reflection, a slightly imperfect composition — anything that signals *presence.*

Your audience connects with presence, not perfection.
They don't need you to look perfect; they need to feel you were *there.*

Key Takeaways

- People feel visuals before they interpret them.
- Overly polished imagery creates emotional distance.
- Imperfections act as "proof of life."
- Composition, colour and texture should serve emotion, not aesthetics.
- Presence — not perfection — builds visual trust.

Reflection Prompt

Look through your last few visual posts.
Which ones felt "too clean" or "too distant"?
What would happen if you replaced one with something slightly rawer — a photo that feels more lived-in than styled?
Test it. See which version people *feel* more.

Next Chapter: "Story as the Natural Container for Truth" — where we'll explore how to turn ordinary experiences into powerful micro-stories that create emotional recognition, not performance.

Chapter 9: Story as the Natural Container for Truth

Why Facts Don't Stick

You can explain an idea clearly and still have it disappear.
You can give advice that's correct and still have it ignored.

That's because information enters the mind.
But **story enters the body.**

A good story bypasses resistance.
It lets readers *feel* the truth instead of debating it.
And when something is felt, it's remembered.

The Psychology of Story

Humans are narrative creatures.
We make sense of chaos by shaping it into beginnings, middles and endings.
Psychologists call this **narrative identity;** the way we understand ourselves through the stories we tell.

When you post online, your audience doesn't just want information.
They want a role in a story:

"Where am I in this?"
"What does this say about me?"

That's why stories work when explanations don't.
They invite participation.

Micro-Stories Beat Monologues

You don't need sweeping arcs or movie scripts.
You need **micro-stories;** small, honest slices of reality that reveal a human truth.

- *A sentence of surprise.*
- *A detail of struggle.*
- *A moment of realisation.*

Each one creates recognition: *"I've felt that."*

The trick is not to dramatise but to **distil.**
Small stories carry big emotions because they leave room for the reader.

The Open-Loop Principle

Every good story creates tension—a question the reader wants answered.
Psychologists call this the **Zeigarnik effect**: our brains remember unfinished things better than finished ones.

Open a loop early ("Something happened today that changed how I think about work...")
and close it with a payoff that feels earned ("...and it reminded me that effort is more trustworthy than talent.")

This rhythm—curiosity then clarity—keeps attention moving and gives emotion somewhere to land.

The Truth Inside the Story

The goal isn't to tell a story for its own sake.
It's to reveal a **truth that feels lived.**

Ask yourself before posting:

"What's the emotional truth here?"

It could be a moment of frustration, joy, doubt or pride.
State it simply, without decoration.
Readers don't need perfection, they need honesty wrapped in motion.

Story Patterns That Work Every Time

You don't need complex frameworks; just these timeless arcs:

1. **Before → After → Lesson**
   A simple transformation. "I used to think ___ → then ___ → now I see ___."

2. **Tension → Choice → Outcome**
   Shows vulnerability through decision. "I almost gave up → I tried ___ → here's what happened."

3. **Moment → Meaning**
   Starts with a snapshot; ends with reflection. "Yesterday I saw ___ → it reminded me ___."

These work because they mirror how people naturally talk when sharing something that mattered to them.

Tone: Honesty Over Heroics

Avoid "I won" narratives. They close the emotional door. Stories that admit confusion, conflict or imperfection open it.

The reader doesn't admire your flawlessness, they trust your *process.*
End your story not with a triumph, but with **truth plus generosity:**

> "If you're there too, that's okay."

That single sentence turns a post into a mirror.

Practical Cue: The Three Rs

When shaping a story, check for these three Rs:

1. **Real:** Does it come from your lived experience?
2. **Relatable:** Can others see themselves in it?
3. **Reflective:** Does it leave the reader thinking or feeling something new?

If all three are present, the story will land.

Key Takeaways

- Stories bypass logic and activate empathy.
- Micro-stories create recognition faster than long narratives.
- Open loops keep attention; truthful endings create satisfaction.
- Vulnerability builds trust; heroics build distance.
- The best stories end with generosity, not glory.

Reflection Prompt

Think of a recent experience that stayed with you, something small but meaningful.
Write it in three sentences: what happened, how it felt and what it meant.
That's a story worth sharing.

Next Chapter: "When Less (or More) Is Exactly Enough" — where we'll explore rhythm and pacing: how to know when to expand, when to cut and how the shape of your post—not its length—determines whether people stay with you.

Chapter 10 — When Less (or More) Is Exactly Enough

Why We Overthink Length

Everyone worries about whether their post is too long or too short.
You trim sentences, count words, second-guess line breaks.
But length isn't what keeps people reading.
Momentum is.

A short post can feel endless if it drags.
A long one can feel quick if it flows.
Attention follows *rhythm*, not *word count*.

When you stop measuring by size and start listening for pulse, you learn the real craft: shaping emotional energy.

The Rhythm of Attention

Every post has a natural tempo.
You can sense it when you read aloud, where it speeds up, slows and lands.

Neuroscience calls this **entrainment**—our brains sync with the patterns they consume.
When rhythm feels natural, readers unconsciously breathe with

your words.
When rhythm breaks, so does attention.

That's why some posts feel heavy, they're packed too tightly.
Others feel hollow, they move too fast.
Your task is to find the *right density* for the emotion you're expressing.

When Less Is More

Brevity works when the *feeling* is already known.

- A moment of shock.
- A punchline.
- A truth that needs space to echo.

Short posts let silence do the heavy lifting.
They feel confident, like eye contact that doesn't blink.

But minimalism only works when the emotion is strong enough to survive trimming.
Cut words until the heartbeat shows, but not until it dies.

When More Is Just Right

Sometimes the story needs air.
A longer post lets readers *walk* with you through thought, emotion or transformation.

Depth builds trust. It signals care.
But expansion fails when it becomes repetition or defence.
You're not convincing; you're inviting.

Ask yourself mid-draft:

"Am I adding clarity—or just padding comfort?"

If the extra words make the experience richer, keep them.
If they make it safer, cut.

The Psychology of Cadence

The brain loves variety, bursts of tension followed by release. Writers and musicians use the same trick: surprise followed by resolution.

You can shape cadence with:

- **Sentence length:** Alternate bursts of speed and rest.
- **Paragraph breaks:** Let the reader breathe.
- **Whitespace:** Visual rhythm that mimics conversation.

Think of your post like breathing: inhale (detail), exhale (insight).

The Silent Sentence

Sometimes the most powerful line isn't written... it's the pause.
A single line break after an emotional truth forces reflection.
It's how you make meaning stick.

Don't fear empty space.
Silence is texture too.

How to Find the Right Shape

Try this quick calibration:

1. **Write freely.** Don't count words.
2. **Read it aloud once.** Notice where energy dips.
3. **Remove anything you skim while reading your own post.**
4. **Add a pause wherever you feel something.**

That's your natural shape, emotionally precise, not algorithmically optimised.

Practical Cue: The Breath Test

Before posting, take one slow breath while reading your draft aloud.
If you can't finish a sentence before needing another breath, it's too long.
If you breathe twice before you feel anything, it's too short.

Your lungs are the best editor you have.

Key Takeaways

- Attention depends on rhythm, not word count.
- Short posts carry emotion; long posts carry journey.
- Use contrast—speed, space and silence—to keep momentum.

- Trim until emotion shines; expand until meaning lands.
- Your breath is a better guide than any metric.

Reflection Prompt

Choose one of your recent posts.
Read it aloud slowly.
Where did you inhale, laugh or pause?
Mark those points.
Now edit for rhythm, not length.

Next Chapter: "The Fear of Trying (and Failing) Publicly" — where we'll confront perfection paralysis head-on and learn how to experiment safely in public without losing confidence or authenticity.

Chapter 11 — The Fear of Trying (and Failing) Publicly

The Quiet Hesitation

There's a special kind of fear that comes with posting online.
It's not stage fright exactly — it's more like *exposure fright.*
You want to share, but a voice whispers,

> "What if this one doesn't land?"
> "What if I sound naive, repetitive or just... ordinary?"

That fear isn't irrational. It's biological.
Humans are wired for belonging — and public failure *feels* like exile.
But in the digital world, **trying in public is the only path to belonging.**

The silence you fear is the silence everyone starts with.

The Psychology of Exposure

Psychologists call it the **spotlight effect** — the belief that more people notice our mistakes than actually do.
In reality, most people are too busy thinking about their own posts, their own performance, their own spotlight.

The irony is: we're all afraid of being judged by an audience that's also afraid of being judged.

When you realise that, posting becomes less about performing and more about *participating.*
You stop thinking, *"What will they think of me?"* and start asking, *"What conversation do I want to be part of?"*

That shift — from self-protection to self-expression — is the foundation of creative freedom.

Why We Hide Behind Perfection

Perfection feels safe because it delays exposure.
You can't fail if you don't publish.
But that safety quickly turns into paralysis.

Psychologically, this is called **avoidance coping** — when we manage anxiety by avoiding the trigger itself. The problem? Avoidance also avoids growth.

You can't find your voice in silence.
You only find it through *use.*

Every imperfect post you publish is a data point in the story of your becoming.

Every unposted one is just a thought that never learned to breathe.

Failure as Proof of Participation

There's a quiet nobility in public imperfection.
It signals courage.
It says, *"I'm learning where others can see me."*

In behavioural psychology, we know that **exposure reduces fear**.
The more often you face the stimulus (in this case, posting), the less the fear controls you.
The first imperfect post feels terrifying. The tenth feels routine.
The hundredth feels natural.

You don't get comfortable by avoiding judgment.
You get comfortable by *surviving it.*

The Hidden Gift of Transparency

When you show your process — your drafts, your experiments, your "not-sures" — people don't think less of you.
They trust you more.

Transparency builds goodwill and empathy. It turns followers into participants.
When you admit you're testing, you invite others to test too.

That's the power of **public practice** — when your audience becomes your collaborator.
They don't just witness your growth; they help shape it.

How to Experiment Without Fear

1. **Define "failure" loosely.**
   A post that didn't perform isn't failure; it's feedback.

2. **Shrink the stakes.**
   You're not addressing the world — you're talking to *one person who gets it.*

3. **Label your experiments.**
   Try prefacing with "I'm testing something new here..." It disarms judgment and invites curiosity.

4. **Separate identity from outcome.**
   Your post failed, not *you.* The distinction matters.

5. **Review without shame.**
   After a post underperforms, ask:

   - Did it express something true?

   - Did I learn something?

   - Would I post it again knowing what I know now?
     If the answer is yes to any of those, that's success.

The Long-Term Benefit of Small Public Risks

Every imperfect post you share is a small exposure to uncertainty.
Over time, those exposures stack up into emotional resilience.
You stop equating silence with rejection.
You start recognising it as *neutral feedback.*

That's how mastery actually happens — not through grand launches, but through micro-experiments that teach your intuition where real connection lives.

Practical Cue: The "First Draft" Mindset

Before posting, remind yourself:

> "This isn't my masterpiece. It's my next data point."

Masterpieces are accidents that happen when you're too busy practising to notice.

Key Takeaways

- Fear of public failure is universal — and survivable.
- The spotlight effect exaggerates how much people notice.
- Avoidance feels safe but prevents growth.
- Sharing transparently builds trust faster than perfection ever will.
- Courage isn't posting without fear; it's posting *despite* it.

Reflection Prompt

Think of one idea you've hesitated to post.
Write it down, flaws and all.
Now, instead of perfecting it, label it as an *experiment.*
When you publish it, you're not proving worth, you're practising honesty.

Next Chapter: "Variety as a Strategy" — where we'll explore how switching tone, format and rhythm keeps your content vibrant, human and immune to creative stagnation.

Chapter 12 — Variety as a Strategy

When Consistency Turns Into Sameness

Consistency is often misunderstood.
We're told to "stay on brand," "post regularly," "keep the same tone."
But after a while, sameness starts to sound like static.

What was once dependable becomes predictable.
Predictable becomes invisible.

The truth is: humans don't crave constant novelty — but we do crave **living rhythm**.
The brain's attention system rewards *variation within familiarity.*
When something feels like *you* but looks slightly different each time, people lean in.
They recognise your voice but never know quite what you'll say next.

That's what real consistency looks like: identity anchored in evolution.

The Psychology of Variety

Our attention systems thrive on **micro-surprise** — the smallest deviation that renews interest without causing confusion. Neuroscientists call this *optimal novelty.*
Too little variety? Boredom.
Too much? Cognitive overload.

The sweet spot lies in **contrast anchored by coherence**:

> "I know this person, but I haven't seen them like this before."

That moment of recognition-with-a-twist releases dopamine — the brain's "stay curious" signal.
It's the same mechanism that keeps us invested in a story, a song or a relationship:
change, but within trust.

Why Most Feeds Feel Dead

When every post looks and sounds identical, even good ideas vanish.
It's like a song played on one note — technically fine, emotionally flat.

You can tell when someone is trapped in this pattern. Their captions blend together. Their visuals repeat.
Their writing loses playfulness.
Audiences drift — not because the creator got worse, but because they stopped surprising.

To keep people's attention, you don't need new topics.
You need new *angles.*

The Three Dimensions of Creative Variety

1. Format Variety: Change the *form* of your content.

- Write a short post, then follow it with a long reflection.
- Alternate between visuals, text and mixed formats.
- Try an occasional carousel or quote if it fits your tone.

Format variation triggers fresh processing in the brain.
Each shift resets curiosity.

2. Emotional Variety: Change the *temperature* of your tone.

- Warm (supportive, reflective).
- Cool (analytical, instructional)..
- Bright (hopeful, humorous).
- Dark (honest, raw, complex).

Your voice stays coherent, but its emotional shading changes — like light across a single landscape.

3. Perspective Variety: Change the *lens* of your storytelling.

- First-person: "Here's what I learned."
- Second-person: "Here's what you might try."
- Third-person: "Here's what I noticed in others."

Each perspective reveals a different facet of your personality — and invites a different kind of empathy.

How Variety Builds Trust

Variety isn't chaos; it's character.
It shows your audience that you're not performing — you're evolving.

That evolution signals life and life signals reliability.
It says: *"I'm still here, still curious, still experimenting."*

And that matters more than aesthetic consistency.
Audiences don't bond with perfection — they bond with persistence.

Designing a Personal Rhythm

Instead of planning content around topics, plan it around **energy cycles.**
Alternate between these three states:

Cycle	Purpose	Example Post Types
Reflective	Build depth and trust	Stories, insights, lessons learned
Expressive	Build warmth and momentum	Visuals, behind-the-scenes, in-the-moment thoughts
Experimental	Build freshness and curiosity	New formats, tone shifts, thought experiments

Rotate through them like a creative heartbeat.
This keeps your content feeling alive without exhausting you.

Permission to Break Patterns

If something starts to feel routine — break it.
If your captions all start the same way, flip the order.
If you always post with a tidy takeaway, end with a question instead.

Patterns are useful until they become cages.
Surprise yourself first; your audience will follow.

Practical Cue: The "Week of Contrast" Challenge

For one week, try this:

- **Day 1:** A raw story (emotion-driven)
- **Day 2:** A one-line post (minimalism)
- **Day 3:** A photo or sketch (visual honesty)
- **Day 4:** A teaching post (clarity and care)
- **Day 5:** A playful or unexpected post (humour, wit or whimsy)

At the end, reflect: which one *felt* most alive?
That's the direction your creativity wants to grow.

Key Takeaways

- Consistency doesn't mean repetition — it means recognisable evolution.
- The brain rewards micro-surprise: variation anchored in familiarity.
- Format, emotion and perspective are your three levers of variety.
- A healthy creative rhythm alternates reflection, expression and experimentation.
- When your content changes shape, your audience rediscovers you.

Reflection Prompt

Look at your last five posts.
How many look or sound the same?
Which one felt most *alive* to make?
Now plan your next piece to break whatever pattern feels safest.

Next Chapter: "The Courage to Post Anyway" — where we'll close out the experimentation theme by exploring how to publish with confidence, quiet the overthinking voice and build rhythm that outlasts doubt.

Chapter 13 — The Courage to Post Anyway

The Moment Before You Press "Post"

Every creator knows that heartbeat right before hitting "publish."
That small, uncomfortable pause; part excitement, part fear.
It's the quiet voice that says:

> "What if this one flops?"
> "What if no one gets it?"
> "What if I'm just shouting into the void?"

Here's the truth: you might be.
At first, most people are.

But the silence isn't judgment.
It's simply **the time it takes for trust to grow.**

Every audience starts as strangers.
The bridge between you and them is built one post at a time — not through perfection, but through persistence.

The Psychology of Repetition

In behavioural science, there's a concept called **exposure familiarity** — the more people see something, the safer and more trustworthy it feels.
That's why a brand, a name or a message only becomes memorable after repeated exposure.

It's also why your first twenty posts might feel invisible.
You're not failing — you're teaching the world who you are.
You're building cognitive trust, one exposure at a time.

So when doubt whispers, *"This isn't working,"* remember:

> You're still early in the repetition curve.

The Illusion of Validation

Early metrics lie.
They measure reach, not resonance.
The posts that change someone's day rarely announce themselves with numbers.

Think of engagement as a delayed echo.
People read, feel something and carry it quietly until one day they comment:

> "I've been following you for a while. This one really hit."

You'll never see the full reach of your work.
But the invisible part — the people watching silently, learning, feeling seen — is often the largest.

That's why you must **create for impact, not applause.**

The Real Definition of Consistency

Consistency doesn't mean posting every day.
It means **showing up when it's easier not to.**

It's emotional endurance — the decision to create even when validation is low.
Over time, that consistency signals something deeper than content quality: it signals *integrity.*

Audiences trust consistency because it mirrors something they crave — reliability in a noisy world.
When you keep showing up, your voice becomes a landmark.

Courage as Creative Currency

Courage is rarely loud.
It's quiet persistence; the willingness to look foolish today in service of clarity tomorrow.

Psychologists describe courage not as the absence of fear, but as **proceeding in its presence.**
Courage and fear share the same space, but courage moves first.

Every imperfect post is a tiny act of rebellion against silence.
And rebellion, repeated daily, becomes momentum.

When Doubt Feels Heavy

You will have days when the fear wins.
When your drafts folder grows and your confidence shrinks.

Here's what to remember on those days:

1. **Your job is to express, not impress.** Connection starts where performance ends.

2. **The silence is part of the process.** It's not rejection; it's incubation.

3. **Nobody else knows what's "normal."** Everyone's feed is a highlight reel of uncertainty.

4. **Progress isn't visible right away.** The human brain adapts slowly to new ideas — even yours.

5. **You don't need to be fearless.** You just need to be curious enough to keep posting.

Reframing the Fear

Instead of asking,

> "What if it fails?"
> Ask,
> "What might I learn if I try?"

Instead of,

> "What will they think of me?"
> Try,
> "What might this help someone else think about?"

Every time you replace fear with purpose, you shrink its power. That's how courage compounds — not in grand leaps, but in small, repeated choices.

Practical Cue: The 10-Minute Rule

When you feel paralysed by hesitation:

1. Set a timer for 10 minutes.
2. Open your draft.
3. Hit publish before it goes off.

No edits. No second-guessing.
The goal isn't to be perfect — it's to break the spell of hesitation.
The post may not be your best, but it will be *yours.*

And that's enough.

Key Takeaways

- Fear before posting is universal — it's a sign of care, not weakness.
- Trust is built through repeated exposure and consistency.

- Metrics can't measure silent impact.
- Courage is proceeding *with* fear, not without it.
- Every imperfect post builds resilience and connection.

Reflection Prompt

Think of one post you didn't share because you were afraid it wouldn't land.
Open it again.
What truth does it hold that still feels alive?
Start there.
Then, post anyway.

Next Chapter: "The Small Audience Advantage" — where we'll explore why starting small isn't a limitation but an opportunity: the perfect environment to experiment, build depth and create meaningful early connections.

Chapter 14 — The Small Audience Advantage

The Myth of the Big Crowd

Most people dream of going viral.
They imagine the rush of thousands of eyes, hundreds of comments, a feed lighting up with validation.
But those same people quietly envy creators who still have *freedom* — who can post what they want, change directions and experiment without a spotlight watching their every move.

Because here's the truth: a large audience amplifies everything — including mistakes, confusion and creative fatigue.

A small audience doesn't mean you're behind.
It means you're *still in the lab.*

The Psychology of Scale

There's a phenomenon called **Dunbar's Number** — the idea that humans can maintain about 150 meaningful relationships.
Beyond that, connection turns into maintenance.
You stop knowing your audience; you start managing them.

That's why small audiences are magical.
You still have space for *conversation*, not just performance.
You can respond, adapt and grow in real time.

A small audience gives you what big creators miss most: **feed-back loops and freedom.**

Learning in Public, Safely

When your reach is limited, your risk is low.
That's a creative jackpot.

You can:

- Test ideas before anyone's watching.
- Experiment with tone, stories and visuals.
- Find what feels true to you, not what gets the biggest reaction.

Psychologists call this a **low-stakes environment** — conditions that support exploration and confidence-building.
It's how mastery begins: through *safe, visible experimentation.*

Every imperfect post at this stage is a small research project.
Each one teaches you what resonates — without the cost of scrutiny.

The Power of Intimacy

Small audiences aren't passive; they're accessible.
They comment thoughtfully, ask questions, remember your sto-

ries.
That level of intimacy is impossible once you scale.

Use that to your advantage.
Talk *with* your audience, not *at* them.
Ask what they struggle with.
Respond to their comments with genuine care.

Each interaction deposits emotional credit.
You're not just gathering followers — you're building *allies.*

Those first 50 people who truly care?
They become your marketing team, your research group, your cheerleaders.

Micro-Engagement, Macro-Insight

When your audience is small, engagement percentages are high because every response matters.
Ten thoughtful comments teach you more than a hundred likes.

Use your small stage as a laboratory:

- Test multiple post types.
- Experiment with timing and rhythm.
- Note what sparks genuine conversation versus polite applause.

The goal isn't to grow fast. It's to grow **smart.**

By the time your audience expands, you'll have something most large creators lack — *clarity.*

Building Affinity Before Scale

If you want long-term resonance, focus on depth, not reach.
Depth compounds.

Depth is when people quote you in conversation.
When they check your feed even when you don't post.
When they start using your language to explain their own ideas.

That kind of loyalty starts small.
It begins when someone feels *seen*, not sold to.
And that's infinitely easier when your audience still fits inside a coffee shop.

The "Dinner Table" Strategy

Imagine your audience as a dinner table that grows one seat at a time.
At 10 people, you're sharing stories.
At 30, you're hosting discussions.
At 100, you're guiding the energy of a room.

You don't need a stage to lead; you need a table people want to return to.

Every new follower is a guest — not a number.
Your role isn't to impress them.
It's to feed them something *meaningful.*

Key Takeaways

- A small audience gives freedom, feedback and safety for experimentation.

- Meaningful connection scales poorly — intimacy is a temporary gift, use it well.
- Every post at this stage is research: test, learn, adapt.
- Focus on *depth of trust* before reach.
- Treat your audience like a dinner table, not a stage.

Reflection Prompt

Think about your current audience, however small.
Who are three people you could genuinely connect with this week?
Send them a message, reply to a comment or thank them for being there.
That's how growth begins — one conversation at a time.

Next Chapter: "Breaking the Rules (and When It Works)" — where we'll explore why sometimes doing the exact *opposite* of what's recommended — posting at odd times, ignoring formulas, breaking tone — can create the strongest engagement of all.

Chapter 15 — Breaking the Rules (And When It Works)

The Myth of the Formula

Every few months, a new set of "rules" sweeps through the creative world.
Write hooks this way.
Use this structure.
Post at these times.
Avoid that tone.

But formulas are like training wheels: they help you start moving but hold you back once you've found balance.

If your goal is to sound *human*, repeating the same formulas guarantees you won't.

Rules are useful only until they start muting your curiosity. That's the moment they stop being tools and start being traps.

Why the Brain Craves Pattern — and Rebellion

Humans love patterns. They make the world predictable. That's why best practices spread quickly: they work *for a while*.

But the same brain that loves pattern also loves **pattern interruption;** small, deliberate violations that jolt attention and reset curiosity.

When something feels slightly off — a broken rhythm, a reversed expectation, an unfinished thought — our brains light up.
We lean forward, trying to make sense of the disruption.

That's the art of breaking rules well: doing it **with intention, not accident.**

Breaking the Hook Rule

You've heard: "The first line must grab attention."
True — but only if your reader needs to be grabbed.

Sometimes, calm is more compelling than drama.
A quiet opening — *"Something strange happened in my kitchen this morning."* — creates intimacy instead of spectacle.

Other times, starting mid-thought — *"I was wrong about all of this."* — draws people in through vulnerability, not volume.

The point isn't to *ignore* hooks, but to *redefine* what hooking feels like.
Curiosity doesn't always come from noise.
It often comes from honesty.

Breaking the Format Rule

You've been told to keep things short.
But sometimes, people crave depth.

Long posts feel indulgent when they wander, but they feel *nourishing* when every paragraph earns its place.
And short posts can fail if they feel thin rather than distilled.

So how do you know which to choose?
Ask:

> "Does this idea need space to breathe, or space to echo?"

If it needs breath, expand.
If it needs echo, compress.

That's rhythm, not rebellion.

Breaking the Visual Rule

Perfect framing. Perfect lighting. Perfect composition.
All correct — and sometimes all wrong.

A photo slightly out of focus can feel immediate.
A candid frame can feel more trustworthy than a studio shot.

If your post's emotion is *raw*, match it visually.
A perfect image can dilute imperfection.
A messy one can *amplify* it.

Breaking the Tone Rule

Tone is where your voice truly matures.
You'll be told to "pick a lane" — funny or serious, emotional or

informative.
But human beings aren't one tone; we're orchestras.

A single post can start playful, turn reflective and end profound.
Those tonal shifts create *emotional dimension*.
The brain recognises it as *life*, not script.

Consistency of **intent**, not tone, is what binds your work together.
Your reader should always feel you — even when your mood changes.

The Science of Intentional Disruption

Research on memory formation shows that we remember the "oddballs" — moments that break pattern just enough to feel distinct.
It's called the **von Restorff effect.**

When your post includes one intentional disruption — a shorter line, an abrupt ending, a one-word paragraph — you make it *memorable* without confusing people.

That's what "breaking the rules" means in practice: **injecting surprise without losing sense.**

When Rule-Breaking Backfires

There's a difference between **artistic disruption** and **confusion.**

Breaking rules works when it:

- Feels intentional, not sloppy.

- Serves emotion, not ego.
- Invites curiosity, not chaos.

If you break a rule and your reader says, *"Interesting,"* that's good.
If they say, *"Wait, what just happened?"* that's not rebellion — that's noise.

The Permission Principle

You earn the right to break rules by understanding them first. Mastery precedes mischief.

Once you know why a technique works, you can subvert it gracefully.
That's when your posts stop following trends and start *creating* them.

Practical Cue: The Rule Reversal Exercise

1. List three "best practices" you've been told to follow.
2. For each, write one post that deliberately breaks it.
    - If you always start with a hook, start with calm.
    - If you always use an image, use none.
    - If you always teach, just tell a story.
3. Notice what happens — both in engagement *and* how it felt to make.

That feeling of freedom? That's creative authenticity resurfacing.

Key Takeaways

- Rules are helpful until they mute curiosity.
- The brain loves small, intentional disruptions.
- Surprise strengthens memory and emotional connection.
- Rule-breaking succeeds when it serves the story.
- Mastery gives you permission to improvise.

Reflection Prompt

Which "best practice" feels most restrictive right now?
Try reversing it for one post.
Don't aim for perfection — aim for discovery.
Sometimes the post that breaks every rule becomes the one that finally *feels* like you.

> **Next Chapter: "Sustaining the Practice"** — where we'll explore how to build a long-term rhythm of creating and sharing without burning out, losing joy or over-editing the humanity out of your work.

Chapter 16 — Sustaining the Practice

The Slow Burn of Creative Work

Posting consistently isn't hard because of time.
It's hard because of *emotion.*

At first, you're energised — full of ideas, momentum and curiosity.
But over time, the pressure to keep showing up starts to feel like weight instead of flow.
You begin to measure yourself by output, not expression.

That's when many people quietly stop.

The truth is, creative sustainability isn't about discipline.
It's about *designing a rhythm that humanity can survive.*

The Psychology of Consistency

In behavioural science, there's a concept called **automaticity** — the point where a repeated action becomes effortless.
It's not about willpower; it's about cues and emotion.

You don't need to post *daily*.
You need a *consistent emotional context* that makes posting feel natural.

That means:

- Setting a small, reliable ritual around your creativity.
- Making your posting process frictionless.
- Rewarding yourself for showing up, not for results.

Consistency grows not from pressure, but from permission.

Rituals Over Routines

Routines are mechanical. Rituals are meaningful.
A routine says, "I must."
A ritual says, "I get to."

Before posting, try something grounding:

- Make coffee.
- Reread an old post that mattered.
- Walk for five minutes.

The ritual isn't about efficiency — it's about emotional rhythm. When you approach creation from calm curiosity, your work carries that energy with it.

Your audience feels it. So do you.

Managing the Creative Cycle

Every creator moves through the same repeating loop:

1. **Excitement:** New ideas, inspiration, curiosity.
2. **Effort:** Execution, focus, experimentation.
3. **Evaluation:** Reflection, self-doubt, comparison.
4. **Recovery:** Rest, disengagement, space to refill.

Most people get stuck in Stage 3 — *evaluation* — and mistake it for failure.
But it's actually part of the cycle.

The trick is to design your rhythm around this loop instead of fighting it.

When your energy dips, don't force output — shift into input.
Listen, read, notice. Let life refill the well.
That's still creative work.

Rest as Strategy

In cognitive science, **incubation** is the period when ideas mature below awareness.
Stepping away doesn't mean you've stopped creating — it means your subconscious has started.

Sometimes the most productive thing you can do for your content is nothing at all.
You're not abandoning your practice. You're letting it breathe.

Creativity needs both tension and release.
Rest is what makes the next spark possible.

How to Avoid Burnout

1. **Post less often than you think you should.** You'll gain longevity, clarity and enthusiasm.

2. **Separate identity from performance.** You are not your metrics. You are your *momentum.*

3. **Create in batches; post in rhythm.** Capture when you're inspired. Schedule when you're calm.

4. **Embrace imperfection early.** The more you chase flawlessness, the shorter your creative life becomes.

5. **Protect private creativity.** Not every idea has to be shared. Some deserve to stay just yours.

The "Three-Mode" Framework

Think of your creative system as having three gears:

Mode	Purpose	Energy Level
Create Mode	Generate freely, explore ideas	High, playful
Refine Mode	Edit and shape for clarity	Focused, thoughtful
Rest Mode	Step away, refill mentally	Low, reflective

Sustainability isn't about staying in Create Mode all the time — it's about moving gracefully between them.

When you stop punishing yourself for resting, your creativity starts regenerating on its own.

Celebrating Small Signals

You won't always get big feedback.
But you'll get small signals: a thoughtful comment, a private message, a friend quoting your post in conversation.

Those moments are proof that your voice is working — even quietly.
Keep a "signal file": a note or document where you store these small bits of encouragement.
It's your creative memory bank — a reminder that connection is cumulative.

Practical Cue: The Rhythm Audit

Once a month, ask yourself:

- Which parts of posting drain me?
- Which parts energise me?
- What feels forced? What feels natural?

Adjust your process to make the energising parts easier and the draining parts rarer.
That's how you create a rhythm that can last years instead of months.

Key Takeaways

- Consistency grows from emotion, not obligation.
- Rituals create meaning; routines create fatigue.
- Creative cycles require recovery as much as output.
- Rest is not absence — it's incubation.
- Design your rhythm to honour how creativity actually works.

Reflection Prompt

What does "sustainable" creativity look like for *you*?
Describe one small ritual, boundary or shift that could make your practice lighter — and start it tomorrow.

Next Chapter: "From Engagement to Affinity" — where we'll move from individual posts to long-term connection: how consistent, human communication transforms casual interaction into genuine loyalty and shared identity.

Chapter 17 — From Engagement to Affinity

The Difference Between Reaction and Relationship

A "like" isn't loyalty.
A comment isn't connection.
A share isn't trust.

They're *signals* — fleeting moments of acknowledgement — but they're not the goal.

Affinity is what happens *after* engagement.
It's when someone starts thinking of you not just as a content creator, but as part of their internal world.
Your ideas, tone and energy become familiar — even comforting.

They no longer interact because you posted something *new.*
They interact because you've become part of their *story.*

The Psychology of Belonging

Humans are wired for affiliation.
In social psychology, **the need to belong** is one of the strongest

motivational forces we have.
It drives everything from brand loyalty to friendships.

What people truly crave online isn't more information — it's **identity affirmation**.
They seek voices that remind them of who they want to be or how they want to feel.

That's how affinity forms: not through frequency, but through **resonant emotional consistency.**
You become a reference point for a feeling they want more of — calm, curiosity, hope, honesty, courage.

You're not just posting; you're modelling a worldview.

How Affinity Begins

Affinity doesn't start with strategy.
It starts with *emotional resonance repeated over time.*

It grows through these three layers:

1. **Recognition** — "I see myself in this."
2. **Reliability** — "They keep showing up the same way."
3. **Resonance** — "This voice feels like part of who I am."

Each layer takes time and vulnerability.
You can't accelerate trust — but you can **nurture predictability.**

When people know the emotional texture of your work, they start to feel *safe* returning to it.

The Emotional Palette of a Brand

Every creator has an emotional palette — the set of feelings their work consistently evokes.
Some creators make people laugh.
Others make them think, reflect or feel calm.

Your palette isn't what you *say,* it's what you *reliably make people feel.*

Ask yourself:

> "If someone scrolled through my last ten posts,
> what emotion would they associate with me?"

That's your current palette.
You can expand or refine it intentionally — but it must stay authentic.
Forced positivity feels fake. So does forced depth.
Your audience feels your energy as much as your words.

Affinity Over Virality

Virality is exposure.
Affinity is belonging.

Viral moments give you reach.
Affinity gives you *roots.*

Virality ends when the trend fades.
Affinity endures because it's emotional, not situational.

Most creators chase reach, then try to retrofit connection.
The smarter path is the opposite: build depth first.
Depth compounds, reach doesn't.

When people trust you emotionally, algorithms start following *them.*

Signals of Affinity

You'll know you're building affinity when you see signs like these:

- People quote your ideas in their own words.
- Comments shift from "Great post!" to "This reminds me of when I..."
- Followers mention your work in DMs or offline conversations.
- Your posts start to spark *their* content.

Affinity means your voice has become a mirror — they see themselves through your lens.

That's the quiet success most creators overlook.

Cultivating Affinity Intentionally

1. **Speak with emotional clarity.**
   Know what your voice represents. Be consistent in tone and intent.

2. **Reward attention with depth.**
   Don't just thank your audience — invite them closer.

Ask, "What did this make you think about?"

3. **Create rituals of belonging.**
   It could be a recurring theme, a phrase or a visual motif — something that signals, *"You're part of this."*

4. **Show growth transparently.**
   People bond more deeply when they witness your evolution.

5. **Protect emotional integrity.**
   Never fake resonance. Trust built on manipulation fractures easily.

Affinity is grown through **emotional repetition, not mechanical frequency.**

Why This Matters More Than Ever

In a world saturated with information, *belonging* has become the most valuable form of engagement.
People don't just want to consume. They want to **connect through content** — to share, discuss and align.

Creators who build affinity become *trusted filters.*
They simplify the noise, offer calm in chaos and remind people that honesty still exists online.

That's a legacy.
And it starts one small post at a time.

Practical Cue: The "Three-Post Resonance Check"

Look at your last three posts and ask:

1. What feeling do they share?
2. What feeling is missing?
3. Which post best represents how I want people to feel when they see my name?

That's your emotional signature.
Write from there.

Key Takeaways

- Belonging, not virality, drives sustainable connection.
- Affinity grows through emotional reliability and resonance.
- Your "emotional palette" defines how your audience feels in your presence.
- Repetition of emotional truth is more powerful than variation of tactics.
- People don't just follow content — they follow identity alignment.

Reflection Prompt

Think of a creator whose posts feel like *home.*
What emotional consistency makes them magnetic?
How could your own content carry that same feeling — in your own way?

Next Chapter: "The Timeless Post" — where we'll explore how to craft content that stays relevant long after it's published: how to make posts that age well, travel far and continue resonating with future readers.

Chapter 18 — The Timeless Post

Why Some Posts Never Expire

You've seen them — those rare posts that resurface months later, still shared, still quoted, still true.
They weren't built for a moment; they were built for meaning.

Timeless posts don't depend on timing, platform or trend.
They depend on **human constants** — emotions, truths and patterns that never go out of style.

While trends chase novelty, timeless work captures *recognition.*
It reminds people of something they've always known but rarely hear said aloud.

That's the secret: *timeless content doesn't teach something new; it clarifies something real.*

The Psychology of Timelessness

Cognitive psychology tells us that memory thrives on **emotional simplicity** and **universal themes.**
When content connects to enduring human drives — safety, belonging, love, purpose, creativity, fairness — it feels evergreen.

These are the anchors of the human experience, unchanged by time or technology.

A timeless post isn't a viral hit.
It's a quiet companion — it stays relevant because it speaks to something people will always feel:

> "This will still be true in ten years."

The Anatomy of a Timeless Post

Timeless posts share three invisible traits:

1. **Emotional Universality**
   They're built around feelings everyone recognises — frustration, hope, self-doubt, pride, gratitude, renewal.
   Example: "You're not behind. You're just building in silence."
   Simple, empathetic, universal.

2. **Linguistic Simplicity**
   They use language that feels conversational, not topical.
   Buzzwords date content; truth preserves it.
   "Authentic," "viral," "growth hack" will age.
   "Human," "honest," "connection" won't.

3. **Reflective Depth**
   They invite readers to look inward.
   Timeless content doesn't demand reaction; it inspires reflection.

It asks, "What does this mean to you?" instead of "Do you agree?"

Why Truth Ages Well

Trends are external.
Truth is internal.

Posts grounded in truth — something you've lived, not learned — retain power because they carry **emotional credibility.**

When people can *feel* that you've earned the insight you're sharing, they trust it.
That trust survives shifts in algorithms, aesthetics and audiences.

Timelessness, then, is a byproduct of **integrity.**
If you wrote it honestly, it will stay relevant, even when everything else changes.

Designing for Longevity

To write something that lasts, focus less on reach and more on **relevance over time.**

Ask yourself:

1. Will this matter next year?

2. Does this depend on a current event or on a timeless emotion?

3. Could someone new to me, five years from now, still feel this truth?

If the answer is yes, that's timeless.

It's the difference between a flash and a flame.

Timeless vs. Timely

Timely posts ride waves.
Timeless posts create currents.

Timely Content	Timeless Content
Anchored to a moment	Anchored to a truth
Uses current language	Uses emotional language
Designed for reaction	Designed for reflection
Rises quickly, fades fast	Grows slowly, endures long

Both matter.
Timely content gets attention.
Timeless content earns *affection.*

The healthiest creative rhythm uses both, posting for today while planting seeds for tomorrow.

The Role of Voice in Timeless Work

Your tone determines whether your message endures.
Writing in your *true voice* — one that isn't mimicking trends — automatically future-proofs your work.

When people look back, the posts that age best sound like *people*, not marketing.
They speak from curiosity, compassion or conviction.

Trends fade when language ossifies; truth lasts because emotion doesn't expire.

The Echo Effect

Timeless posts create **echoes** — people save them, quote them, re-share them later.
Those echoes multiply over time.

That's how creators outlast algorithms: their words travel through memory, not just feeds.
They become reference points — the sentences people repeat when their own words fail.

That's not virality.
That's legacy.

Practical Cue: The Campfire Test

Before posting, ask:

> "If I said this aloud around a campfire, would people nod in recognition — or just scroll past?"

If it would make someone look up and say, *"I needed that,"* it's timeless.

If it only makes sense in the current context, it's temporary.
Create for the campfire. Not the feed.

Key Takeaways

- Timeless content draws from universal emotions, not temporary trends.
- Simplicity and sincerity make messages endure.
- Truth ages well because it feels earned, not engineered.
- Combine timely energy with timeless depth for sustainable connection.
- The goal isn't to go viral today — it's to stay valuable tomorrow.

Reflection Prompt

Revisit your most meaningful post.
Would it still resonate if someone read it a year from now?
If yes, that's timeless.
If not, what truth could you distil from it that *would* last?

Next Chapter: "The Human Algorithm" — the penultimate chapter, exploring how to stay visible and connected in an ever-changing digital world by leaning on timeless human principles, not platform mechanics.

Chapter 19 — The Human Algorithm

The Illusion of Control

Every creator wants to "understand the algorithm."
They want to know when to post, what format wins, which keywords trigger reach.

But algorithms are like weather systems — constantly shifting, impossible to fully predict.
And chasing them traps you in a cycle of exhaustion and dependency.

The truth is: no one truly controls digital visibility.
But everyone influences *human visibility.*

There's another algorithm running in parallel — older, stronger and far more consistent.
It's the one in your reader's mind.

That's the **Human Algorithm** — the emotional system that decides what we notice, trust and share.
And it hasn't changed for thousands of years.

The Psychology Behind Every Platform

Strip away the logos and layouts and every platform is built on the same timeless mechanics of attention:

- **Curiosity:** We seek what we don't yet understand.
- **Recognition:** We engage when something feels familiar.
- **Emotion:** We react when something makes us *feel.*
- **Reciprocity:** We give when we've been given to.

Every like, comment or share is just a digital expression of these ancient instincts.

So instead of asking, *"What does the algorithm want?"*
Ask, *"What does the person behind the screen need right now?"*

Because every algorithm, in the end, is just a mirror of that.

The Feedback Loop of Humanity

When your post connects deeply — when someone feels seen, inspired or relieved — they react.
Their reaction signals to the system: "This matters."
The system amplifies it.

The pattern seems algorithmic, but it's actually **empathic.**

Human reaction drives machine amplification, not the other way around.
That's why authenticity still wins — even in a world optimised

for manipulation.
The system can't fake sincerity; it can only echo it.

The Emotional Ranking System

Think of engagement not as metrics, but as messages:

Reaction	What It Means
Like	"I agree."
Comment	"I relate."
Share	"This represents me."
Save	"I'll need this again."
Message	"This changed me."

Each is a deeper rung on the ladder of emotional investment. The deeper you go, the less algorithms matter — because people become the algorithm.

They start spreading your work through trust, not traffic.

How to Speak to the Human Algorithm

1. **Start with empathy.**
   Don't write to be seen; write to make someone feel seen.

2. **Simplify the signal.**
   Attention is fragile. Speak clearly and sincerely, without noise.

3. **Be emotionally consistent.**

People come back to what feels safe and familiar.

4. **Share stories, not status updates.**
   The human brain organises meaning through narrative, not data.

5. **Reward emotion with honesty.**
   When people engage, don't optimise — acknowledge. Connection is the real feedback loop.

The Limits of Data

Data tells you *what* happened, not *why.*
It can measure behaviour, but not feeling.
It can predict trends, but not trust.

When you focus only on numbers, you start posting for outcomes instead of *people.*
And people can sense that — instantly.

The Human Algorithm rewards energy, not efficiency.
You can't automate warmth.
You can only express it.

Trust as the Ultimate Metric

Metrics fluctuate. Trust compounds.
When someone trusts your voice, your message bypasses the platform altogether.

They'll seek your content out, even if it never reaches their feed.
That's what every creator is truly building — not an audience, but **an affinity network.**

A group of people who don't just consume your work, but carry it forward in conversation.

That's the only algorithm worth optimising for.

Practical Cue: The "One Reader" Test

Before posting, ask:

> "If this post reached only one person — and it helped them — would it still be worth it?"

If yes, publish it.
That's how timeless impact starts — one genuine human response at a time.

Key Takeaways

- The real algorithm is human attention, emotion and reciprocity.
- Authentic connection drives amplification — not the other way around.
- Empathy, clarity and consistency beat tactics over time.
- Data explains outcomes but can't predict meaning.
- Trust, not reach, is the metric that endures.

Reflection Prompt

What kind of feeling do you want your posts to leave behind?
Peace? Energy? Curiosity? Relief?
Write that word somewhere visible.
That's your new algorithm.

Next Chapter (Final): "The Imperfect Conclusion" — a closing reflection tying everything together: imperfection as a creative compass, humanity as strategy and interaction as the art of being *felt*.

Chapter 20 — The Imperfect Conclusion

The Thread That Runs Through It All

You started this book looking for ways to make your posts resonate — to get more likes, more comments, more interaction.

But what you've really been learning isn't how to get *reactions.* It's how to be *felt.*

Behind every principle — emotional texture, goodwill, variety, courage, rhythm — there's been a single through-line: **your humanity is the strategy.**

The best posts aren't those that look the most professional. They're the ones that feel most *alive.*

The Courage to Be Seen Imperfectly

We often think of imperfection as a flaw — something to fix before sharing.
But imperfection is proof of life.
It's the heartbeat that tells the reader, *someone real made this.*

When you share something unpolished, you're not showing carelessness — you're showing courage.

Courage to be unfinished in public.
Courage to let people see the process instead of the product.

And in that courage, people see themselves.

Because deep down, we're all unfinished too.

Why Interaction Is Emotional, Not Mechanical

Every click, comment or share is just a small human echo, someone saying, *"I felt that."*
You can't force it.
You can only create the conditions where it might happen: honesty, generosity, rhythm and care.

That's the art of interaction — not manipulating psychology, but aligning with it.

When you post from truth, people don't just interact with your *content.*
They interact with your *energy.*

Your Audience Doesn't Need Perfection

They don't need polished phrasing, flawless lighting or unshakable confidence.
They need presence.

They want to know that behind the screen is someone real — someone who forgets words mid-sentence, who changes their mind, who posts something half-formed because it mattered in that moment.

They don't need you to be perfect.
They need you to be *in progress.*

That's how you give others permission to show up imperfectly too.

Why Imperfection Lasts Longer Than Perfection

Perfect content belongs to the moment it was created.
Imperfect content belongs to every moment after.

Because it ages with you.
It grows as your readers grow.
It keeps reflecting what's real.

Perfection locks your work in time.
Imperfection keeps it alive.

From Interaction to Impact

Interaction isn't the goal — it's the beginning.
Every small engagement is a door to something larger:

- A conversation.
- A shared idea.
- A shift in someone's perspective.

That's the hidden miracle of imperfect posts: they ripple quietly through people's lives, often in ways you'll never see.

And if you can accept that — that the most important impact might be invisible — you'll post with more peace, more honesty and more joy.

A Return to Why

You didn't start creating to hack systems or chase metrics. You started because you had something to say, something to offer, something to connect.

That impulse — to reach across the void and say, *"Does anyone else feel this?"* — is the most human instinct there is.

Everything in this book has simply been a way to honour that instinct better.

To make your reach more resonant.
To make your voice more *you.*

The Creative Contract

Here's the only promise you need going forward:

> "I will post as a person first, creator second.
> I will value connection over performance.
> I will trust imperfection to carry truth."

Keep that promise and every post — no matter how small — will matter.
Maybe not to everyone. But to *someone.*

And that's enough.

Practical Cue: The One-Post Reset

When you feel overwhelmed by advice, algorithms or doubt, return to this question:

> "What would I post if I knew I couldn't get it wrong?"

Write that.
That's your next imperfect post.

Key Takeaways

- Imperfection is not the enemy of connection — it's the engine of it.
- Interaction is emotional before it's mechanical.
- Authenticity isn't a tactic; it's the only timeless strategy.
- Presence beats polish. Honesty beats performance.
- You don't need to create perfect posts. You just need to keep creating *honest* ones.

Closing Reflection

The next time you post — whether it's a single line, a story or an image — remember:
You're not posting to impress.
You're posting to express.

You're not trying to look flawless.
You're trying to look *alive.*

And in a world that increasingly feels automated, that's the most powerful thing you can be.

Appendices

Appendix A – The Imperfect Posts Framework

Use this as your quick reference — a pre-post checklist for creating content that feels *human, resonant and alive.*

1. Presence Before Perfection

Before posting, ask:

- Does this sound like a person or a performance?
- Does it express something real, even if it's rough?

If it sounds polished but lifeless, loosen it.

2. The HEART Framework

A simple lens to evaluate your post before hitting publish:

Element	Question to Ask	Psychological Trigger
H — Honesty	Is this emotionally true, not just technically correct?	Authenticity & vulnerability
E — Empathy	Does it meet the reader where they are?	Belonging & recognition
A — Affection	Does it give before it asks?	Reciprocity & goodwill
R — Rhythm	Does it move with emotional variety?	Curiosity & attention
T — Texture	Does it sound lived, not written?	Trust through imperfection

If your post hits three or more of these five, it's ready.
If it hits all five, it's *alive.*

3. The 3-Second Test

Look at your post and ask:

> "Will someone *feel* something within three seconds?"

If the answer is no, edit for **emotion**, not wording.

4. The 80% Rule

Stop at 80% polished.
The last 20% rarely adds clarity — only caution.

5. The One-Reader Mindset

Imagine your post is for one specific person — someone who would actually *care.*
Write to them. Forget the rest.

Appendix B – The Psychology Behind Engagement

A quick reference for the key biases and emotional triggers woven through this book.

Principle	**Description**	**Why It Matters for Posts**
Reciprocity	When people receive value, they want to return it.	Give emotional or informational value freely.
Identity Signaling	People engage with content that reinforces who they are or want to be.	Align posts with shared values and language.
Emotional Contagion	Emotions spread through tone and rhythm.	Write with authentic emotion; readers will mirror it.
Curiosity Gap	People engage to close the gap between what they know and what they want to know.	Start with tension, deliver with clarity.
Social Proof	We trust what others find meaningful.	Share genuine feedback or real stories, not vanity metrics.
Fluency Effect	The easier something is to process, the more we trust it.	Use plain language and simple structure.
Novelty Bias	We notice what breaks pattern.	Inject small surprises or tonal shifts.
Ben Franklin Effect	We grow fonder of people we've helped.	Ask questions or invite small contributions.
Handmade Effect	Imperfections signal human effort.	Keep small quirks, handwritten notes and unscripted moments.

Appendix C – The Reader's Practice Plan

A 30-day roadmap to help you integrate the *Imperfect Posts* philosophy into real creative rhythm.

Week 1: Presence

- Post something unpolished but honest.
- Focus on tone, not topic.
- Read your post out loud before publishing.

Goal: Break the perfection loop.

Week 2: Emotion

- Identify one feeling you want each post to evoke.
- Use variety — joy, reflection, gratitude, frustration.
- Experiment with rhythm and pacing.

Goal: Build emotional texture.

Week 3: Reciprocity

- Create one post that gives: a story, a tip, a reflection or comfort.

- Ask for nothing.
- Watch how people naturally reciprocate.

Goal: Generate goodwill through generosity.

Week 4: Affinity

- Notice who interacts most sincerely.
- Engage back — personally and meaningfully.
- Share a reflection on what you've learned.

Goal: Turn engagement into connection.

By the end of 30 days, you'll have rhythm, confidence and a clearer emotional fingerprint — your *imperfect style.*

Appendix D – The Timeless Checklist

Use this to test whether a post will endure beyond the moment:

- It speaks to a universal emotion.
- It could make sense five years from now.
- It sounds like something you'd still stand by later.

- It doesn't rely on trends or jargon.
- It feels like a conversation, not a campaign.

If it passes three or more, it's likely timeless.
If it passes all five, it's not just a post. It's a keepsake.

Appendix E – Glossary of Key Ideas

Affinity:
Emotional loyalty — when followers start identifying with your message, not just reacting to it.

Emotional Texture:
The variation of tone, pacing and rhythm that makes your content feel alive.

Goodwill:
The invisible trust earned by generosity and authenticity.

Micro-Story:
A small, truthful anecdote that communicates a universal feeling.

The Human Algorithm:
The timeless psychology behind why people notice, care and share — curiosity, recognition and empathy.

Timeless Post:
A post anchored in truth and emotion rather than timing or trend.

Appendix F – The Psychology of Digital Reactions

Why This Matters

Every click, comment, or share isn't random, it's an emotional micro-expression.
Each action corresponds to a *different kind of connection* your audience feels toward your content. Understanding these psychological cues allows you to design posts that evoke the right type of participation — not through manipulation, but through empathy.

1. Likes – Instant Recognition

Psychology:
A *like* is the lowest-friction, highest-frequency response. It signals *recognition,* the viewer sees themselves, their beliefs, or their aesthetic reflected in your post. It's the brain's "me too" reaction.

Why people like:

- To affirm shared identity or values (social belonging).
- To support the creator passively (reciprocity).
- To acknowledge emotional tone (emotional mirroring).

How to invite more likes:

- Use clear, emotionally legible tone (warmth, gratitude, truth).
- Share relatable micro-moments ("ever have one of those

days…”).

- End with a subtle pause or line that lets readers nod silently.

Likes thrive on recognition, not requests.

Angle to take:
Use likes as *pulse checks,* signals that your message was emotionally *seen*, even if not deeply discussed.

2. Comments – Emotional Engagement

Psychology:
A comment takes cognitive effort. It signals *activation*: your post made someone *think or feel* enough to join the conversation.

Why people comment:

- To express agreement or challenge (identity signaling).
- To share a personal story (empathy overflow).
- To connect directly with the creator (social reciprocity).

How to invite more comments:

- Ask open-ended, emotional questions: “What does that look like for you?”
- Share stories that create space for others’ experiences.
- Respond meaningfully, comments multiply when peo-

ple see real conversation.

Angle to take:
Frame your posts as *campfire starters,* not declarations, but discussions.
The best prompts invite *interpretation*, not confirmation.

3. Shares – Identity & Alignment

Psychology:
Sharing is high-commitment. It's a *public endorsement* that says, "This represents me."
It triggers both **identity signaling** and **social reciprocity** — people share what makes them look insightful, kind, or self-aware.

Why people share:

- It reinforces their personal brand or worldview.
- It expresses empathy or aspiration ("this says what I feel").
- It helps others ("someone I know needs to read this").

How to invite more shares:

- Write sentences that are emotionally quotable.
- Offer distilled clarity, ideas people can proudly stand behind.
- Use phrases that carry emotional truth ("You're not behind. You're just building quietly.").

Angle to take:
Create *shareable empathy.*
Posts that help people *say what they can't yet articulate* are the ones most likely to travel.

4. Saves – Reflection & Depth

Psychology:
Saving is introspective. It means your post wasn't for the *now*, but for *later.*
This reflects **cognitive resonance** — people sense ongoing value.

Why people save:

- The content is actionable or insightful (mental utility).
- It evokes reflection (emotional depth).
- It feels too valuable to lose (scarcity effect).

How to invite more saves:

- Offer clarity through frameworks, steps, or truths worth revisiting.
- Include phrases like "You'll want to come back to this."
- Design rhythmically; clean layout, concise takeaways.

Angle to take:
Saves are trust signals.
When someone saves your work, it's because they've *decided you're worth remembering.*

5. Reposts – Advocacy & Social Proof

Psychology:
A repost transforms engagement into *advocacy.*
People aren't just agreeing, they're *borrowing your voice* to speak for them.

Why people repost:

- To signal alignment or admiration (social identity).
- To support your work publicly (reciprocity + goodwill).
- To amplify a message that serves their own community.

How to invite more reposts:

- Center universal truths that transcend niches.
- Make visuals simple and portable (carousels, quotes, frameworks).
- Acknowledge community: "If this helps you, pass it on."

Angle to take:
Reposts thrive on generosity.
When your message feels collective, not proprietary, people carry it forward.

6. Direct Messages – Intimacy & Trust

Psychology:
DMs represent the deepest emotional reaction, the *private echo.* It's where people go when they've been moved beyond public comment.

Why people DM:

- To share resonance privately (emotional safety).
- To express gratitude or curiosity.
- To test relational closeness (personal connection).

How to invite more DMs:

- Write posts that feel personal but incomplete ("I'm still thinking about this...").
- Share lessons that feel whispered, not announced.
- Add a quiet call-in: "If this hit home, message me, I'd love to hear."

Angle to take:
DMs are not metrics, they're *relationships.*
They signal that your words reached past the screen into real trust.

7. Clicks & Follows – Curiosity & Continuity

Psychology:
A click or follow means, "I want more of this energy."

It reflects **anticipated trust** — belief that future content will feel similarly resonant.

Why people click:

- To explore coherence (does your message match your identity?).
- To learn more about the source (credibility building).
- To stay connected to a feeling (emotional reinforcement).

How to invite more clicks/follows:

- Keep your tone consistent across posts and bio.
- Offer depth without oversharing, intrigue over information.
- End posts with quiet bridges: "More reflections like this soon."

Angle to take:
Clicks aren't conversions, they're curiosity signals.
Earn them with coherence, not campaigns.

8. Silence – The Invisible Reaction

Psychology:
Silence isn't absence; it's *processing.*
Many readers engage privately — reflecting, bookmarking, or internalising without response.

Why silence happens:

- Overwhelm (too much content, not enough mental space).
- Emotional resonance that needs time to unfold.
- Lurking affection, they care but rarely react publicly.

How to reframe it:

- Treat silence as incubation, not rejection.
- Keep posting with rhythm and sincerity, not pressure.
- Trust that unseen impact often grows roots later.

Angle to take:
The goal isn't noise, it's nourishment.
You don't need to be heard by everyone; just *felt* by someone.

Final Thought

Every reaction tells a story about **human need** — for recognition, safety, reflection, or belonging.
When you understand that psychology, you stop chasing engagement and start *facilitating connection.*

> Don't ask, "How do I get more likes?"
> Ask, "What emotion am I giving people permission to feel?"

That's what turns interaction into relationship, and posts into presence.

Acknowledgements

To everyone who's ever posted something imperfect... something half-formed, vulnerable or quietly hopeful, thank you.
You're the proof that connection doesn't come from polish; it comes from presence.

To the readers who finish this book and immediately post something *real*:
you're the reason it exists.

Most importantly, to my wife — Skie, my kids — Tamar, Zoe & Asher, and my extended family — John, Donna, Binny, Andy & the rest of the tribe, thanks for your love & support.

Made in the USA
Monee, IL
04 November 2026

67385876R10079